MOUNT ST. HELENS

The Big Blast

by RITA GOLDEN GELMAN

SCHOLASTIC BOOK SERVICES

NEW YORK • TORONTO • LONDON • AUCKLAND • SYDNEY • TOKYO

For Steve, with love

Front cover:
Woodfin Camp/Roger Werth
  © 1980 Longview Daily News
Back cover: Woodfin Camp/© Bill Thompson, 1980
Drawing, page 5, by Ted Hanke
Inside photo credits, page 80

ISBN 0-590-31961-2

12 11 10 9 8 7 6 5 4 3 2 1   2   1 2 3 4 5 6/8

Contents

◀ A serene Mount St. Helens rises above Spirit Lake, in this photo released by the Northern Pacific Railway, years before the eruption. The caption reads: "This eternally snow-crowned peak of the Cascade Range was formerly a volcano. The great, white, symmetrical cone is visible from trains between Seattle and Portland. It is one of the most beautiful mountains in America."

Below
Volcano erupting through its throat or vent. Note how the mountain has been built up with layers of ash and lava.

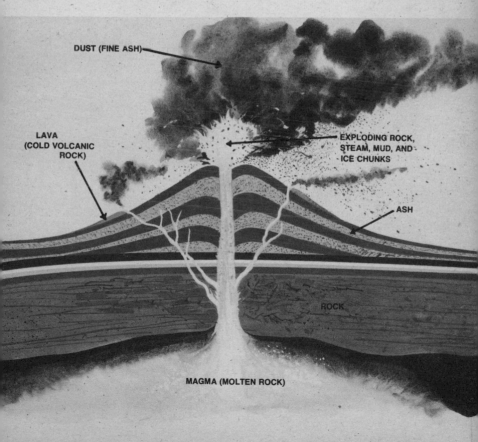

DUST (FINE ASH)

LAVA
(COLD VOLCANIC
ROCK)

EXPLODING ROCK,
STEAM, MUD, AND
ICE CHUNKS

ASH

ROCK

MAGMA (MOLTEN ROCK)

Temporarily quiet. Closeup of Mount St. Helens on March 31, 1980, showing snowy southwest flank of the cone still unstained, although northeast side is coated with ash.

Mount St. Helens Wakes Up

For 123 years, Mount St. Helens volcano, in the state of Washington, had been quiet. Its throat was tightly plugged with rock and ash and ice. Then, on March 20, 1980, an earthquake shook the mountain. In the next week, the mountain rumbled with more than 100 big earthquakes and thousands of small ones.

On March 27, just after noon, a loud noise came from the mountain, a boom that was heard miles away. The volcano began to shoot steam and ash into the air.

"There was crackling, booming, banging, rumbling, and growling," said a sheriff's deputy, stationed near the mountain that night.

The eruption was not a major one. Only the debris at the top of the throat was blown out.

"Small potatoes," said one scientist.

But there was no doubt that Mount St. Helens was waking up. Geologists, people who study the earth, rushed to the mountain to record the awakening.

Over the next weeks, Mount St. Helens coughed and sneezed and rumbled. It spit ice and rocks into the air. It belched steam and gases into the sky.

The look of the mountain began to change. The beautiful, white snow became stained with gray ash. The smooth surface developed big cracks. And a black crater, 200 feet wide, appeared in the summit. (See photo on opposite page.)

The sound of the mountain changed also. Steam squirted through the snow in dozens of places. The earthquakes continued. The small explosions continued. And long rumbles were heard and felt, rumbles that came from inside the mountain. These rumbles meant that hot molten rock, called magma, was moving up the throat of the volcano.

Another view of Mount St. Helens, taken around March 30, 1980, looking straight down at the 200-foot-wide crater, and a second, smaller one at the mountain's top. Later, these two merged into one big crater (see page 12).

The scientists were worried. They knew that Mount St. Helens was unpredictable. At any time the volcano could burst and send hot gases into the air, and walls of mud sliding down the mountain into areas where people lived and worked.

The scientists were not worried that hot lava might pour out of the volcano. (The hot, molten rock is called *magma* when it is inside, *lava* when it comes out.) The magma in the Mount St. Helens volcano is thick, like toothpaste. It can't "pour." But thick magma traps gases and causes giant explosions. The scientists *were* worried about the possibility of explosions.

The scientists alerted the authorities that the volcano was very dangerous. People who lived on the mountain were evacuated from their homes. A danger area, called the Red Zone, was marked off on a map; and only scientists were allowed inside. Barricades were set up on the mountain roads to keep everyone else away.

At first, people were frightened. But, as weeks went by and nothing dramatic happened, they gradually became accustomed to having a volcano in their back yards.

They made jokes about the restless mountain. One man told reporters that he was getting tired of "all those quakes. They're making my false teeth rattle."

People were also getting tired of the disaster predictions. They decided that scientists worry too much. Families began driving and hiking on back roads into the Red Zone — just to get a closer look. Some local folks even sold maps that showed tourists how to avoid the barricades by using the logging roads.

Sightseers' cars are stopped by a police roadblock on March 29, following a minor eruption. Many people hiked in for a closer look.

By mid-May, there was almost a carnival atmosphere surrounding the volcano. People were selling T-shirts that read "I Lava Volcano" and "Mount St. Helens Is Hot."

They sold packets of volcanic ash to the tourists. They mailed the ash to their friends. Postal machines broke down when the envelopes burst and the ash puffed out, clogging the mechanisms.

After a while, the volcano seemed more like a friend than an enemy. In fact, people were rather proud of their volcano. It was, after all, the only sputtering volcano in the 48 connected United States. (There are active volcanoes in Alaska and Hawaii.)

By April 6, the two craters had merged into a single large one, 1,500 feet across. This is a northeast aerial view.

"Everyone secretly hopes," wrote one newspaper, "that Mount St. Helens will put on a big show — not a big China Syndrome core meltdown, but a respectable eruption that will cause the world to admire the performance of one of the youngest of all the volcanic sisters of the beautiful, snow-capped Cascades."

Another newspaper wrote, "A small event . . . would be great. Lots of smoke, lots of steam, and a modest flow of lava. . . ."

The scientists, on the other hand, were much more worried than the people, especially after they noticed the giant lump that was growing on the north slope of the mountain. The lump was half a mile long and half a mile wide, and it was swelling out from the mountain like a huge mosquito bite.

By the middle of May, the lump stuck out more than 300 feet; and it was growing another five feet every day. Scientists explained that the magma was pushing out the north slope like a giant fist inside the mountain.

"Is it going to explode?" asked the local people, the newspaper reporters, the TV broadcasters.

"We don't know," answered the scientists. "All we can do is watch."

Every day they watched and measured. They photographed and recorded. The scientists hoped that they'd get some kind of warning from the mountain if a really big explosion was about to take place.

Throughout the early weeks in May, nothing unusual happened. There were earthquakes, tremors, and occasional spurts of steam, but nothing spectacular. There was nothing that hinted at what was about to happen . . . except maybe the growing lump on the north slope.

The Eruption

May 18, 1980. 5:39 A.M. Sunrise on Mount St. Helens. Birds in search of breakfast are flitting in and out of the giant Douglas fir trees. Some campers notice that the birds seem quieter than usual.

As the sun rises higher, the other forest animals begin their day. Families of black-tailed deer move silently through the forest; their hoofs leave barely a trace in the soft, springy pine needles.

A mountain lion, nearly eight feet long, is perched on a low branch, waiting to pounce on a young deer.

There are big herds of elk, moving together through the trees. A few mountain goats are resting just below the north slope.

There are field mice, snakes, rabbits, coyotes, insects, all going about their morning business, unconcerned about the big bulge on the north side of the mountain. Probably, they are not even aware that it is bulging more each day.

Most of the people who live on the mountain have been evacuated. Yesterday, the people who owned cabins around Spirit Lake were permitted to visit their homes for a few hours. They have convinced the sheriff to let them come back today. They are due to return at 10 A.M.

The only one of the residents who has refused to leave the mountain is Harry Truman, an 84-year-old man who runs a lodge on the edge of Spirit Lake, just down from the north slope.

Every summer Harry's lodge is filled with hikers and campers and kids. Harry loves talking to people, entertaining kids with tales about Mount St. Helens.

When the sheriff came by to tell Harry he had to evacuate, Harry said he wasn't moving.

"I've been on this mountain fifty-four years and I can stick it out another fifty-four," Harry said. "No one knows more about this mountain than Harry, and it don't dare blow on him. I'm staying right here."

Harry Truman, 84, suns himself on the steps of his lodge, located just north of the crater, only a week before the eruption that blasted the area.

So Harry was given special permission to stay.

On the morning of May 18, Harry goes about his usual routine. He rises with the birds. He eats a breakfast of bacon and eggs. He fusses over his 16 cats.

"This mountain and this lake are a part of me and I'm a part of them," Harry had said. "If the mountain goes, I'm going with it." Harry would get his wish.

Harry is not the only person on the mountain this morning. There are others. Just across the lake from Harry's lodge are two people in a camper. Yesterday, they wiggled their way around the roadblocks, along little logging roads. They are pleased and excited to be so close to the volcano, inside the danger zone, where no one is allowed.

Elsewhere, there is an artist with her easel set up. She is painting a picture of the gray peak. Her husband and 14-year-old son have gone for a walk. This family, too, has managed to hike into the Red Zone, hoping to get a better view.

And there are others. Families, couples, young people, old people, loggers, sightseers, press. They all feel a special excitement at being so close to a live volcano. Like Harry Truman, most of them will never leave the mountain.

Across from the north slope of the mountain, a volcano scientist, David Johnston, is peering

David Johnston, volcanologist, labels ash samples. He was monitoring the volcano's activity from an observation post about 5 miles north of the crater on May 18, and reported the blast just before his radio went dead.

at the lump through his binoculars. He is carrying a two-way radio. Later, Johnston plans to talk to the local headquarters of the U.S. Geological Survey in Vancouver, Washington.

On March 28, Johnston had told the press, "We're standing next to a dynamite keg and the fuse is lit. The problem is that no one knows how long the fuse is."

Now, a month and a half later, Johnston is the first one to find out that the fuse is used up. At 8:30, he shouts into his radio, "Vancouver, Vancouver. THIS IS IT!"

They are his last words.

At 8:30 A.M., Mount St. Helens is rattled by an earthquake. Then more earthquakes, smaller ones, shake the tortured mountain. The bulging north slope quivers. The weakened crust that has been holding back the magma begins to slide. In a massive hunk, the rocks, the snow, the ice, the hardened lava that make up the north slope of Mount St. Helens, crash down the mountain.

At 8:32, the mountain blows.

The explosion is heard 200 miles away. It is louder and more powerful than an atom bomb.

The big blast in an aerial view from the west. The ash plume reached over 60,000 feet into the atmosphere.

A gray-black cloud of ash shoots into the air, and the guts of the volcano rocket more than 12 miles into the sky.

Seconds after the cloud shoots up, the north slope explodes out to the side. The heat and force of the blast are unimaginable.

Hundreds of thousands of trees in the direct line of the blast are vaporized or turned into dust. Millions more are skinned of their bark, and branches are lifted like toothpicks into the fury of the exploding volcano.

Thousands of trees across 185 square miles of forestland were instantly leveled by the atom bomb-like blast of Mount St. Helens on May 18.

Spirit Lake disappears. In its place are patches of boiling, steaming, gray liquid and cast-off trees and mud and rock and ash.

Harry Truman's lodge and the dozens of cabins and houses and camps that surrounded Spirit Lake are gone — vaporized or blown to bits or buried in ash more than 40 feet deep.

Further down the mountain, more than 10 miles from the summit, a 10-ton bulldozer is lifted by the blast and carried 1,100 feet through the air. Not far away, a mountain fire truck weighing many tons is thrown more than 1,500 feet, and then it is dumped like a broken toy into a pile of tree trunks.

The people on the mountain are thrown like the trees . . . or smothered in ash . . . or roasted in their cars. It happens quickly. Harry Truman, who loved his mountain more than his life, does not even have time to question his decision to stay.

There is no trace of David Johnston, the geologist who was the first to realize that the mountain was going. Nor is there any trace of his jeep or his trailer. They have disappeared.

The campers, the loggers, the sightseers — they are all gone.

The blast from the north side of the mountain wipes out everything in its path. It levels more than 150 square miles and leaves a gray, empty moonscape.

Car buried in ash contained the body of news photographer Reid Blackburn, one of Mount St. Helens' many victims.

Fumaroles make a desolate moonscape out of beautiful Spirit Lake.

More about the eruption

• Two geologists were flying over the mountain when the north side crumbled. The pilot reported:

"It looked like someone just sliced a straight line right across. . . . Everything north of that line started to ripple and churn up. It did this for about 10 seconds. . . . Then suddenly . . . the north side of the mountain just caved away, slid away. Within a few short seconds a huge blast of ash came right out. . . . That's when I said, 'Let's get out of here.' "

• Other people who saw the eruption saw it from a distance:

"It reminded me of movies where they show the world blowing up."

"It was like an atomic explosion."

"It was like a Bible movie. You felt like falling down on your knees and covering your face."

More about the blast

Comments of people who visited the blast area during the week following the eruption:

- "It looked like we were on another planet."

- "Spirit Lake is a weird and unattractive place. It's Evil Spirit Lake right now."

- "I feel like I've just come back from the moon."

— *Gov. Dixy Lee Ray, Wash.*

- "It was gruesome. It was weird."

- "Nothing was left. It's like a huge vacuum cleaner just sucked everything out of there."

- "It's an evil-looking place for the dead."

- "The moon looks like a golf course compared to what's up there."

— *President Jimmy Carter*

(Above) Path of mudflow and closeup of giant trees torn up by its power. (Below) A soldier searches for possible bodies in a debris- and ash-covered car.

The Mud

The blast was over in minutes. But the mud kept rolling for hours.

The moving wall of mud began as a mixture of shattered mountain and melted ice and snow. Hotter than boiling water, the mud raced down the mountain at a speed of more than 100 miles per hour, gathering more and more of the mountain into its terrifying flow.

It flowed to the low areas, through the valleys, along the stream beds, and into the rivers. It gathered trees and rocks, animals and earth, and people.

Wreckage of bridge *(above)* and houses *(below)* caught in path of mudflow.

The wall of mud, a mile wide, swept through two logging camps, picking up trucks and cars and piles of logs and adding them to the moving mass.

It swept across bridges, yanking them from their moorings and carrying them down the river.

A young man who was camping with a friend on the bank of the Toutle River remembers:

"I woke up and the river just didn't sound the same. All of a sudden I see this wall of logs coming straight at us. I started throwing stuff in the car and I looked down and saw the water around my ankles. Then I looked up and saw what looked like a railroad bridge. It was holding all the logs back in one huge pile.

"And then it started to move. Man, that thing was snapping trees when it came down the river. It was pure havoc. Havoc and a half."

The camper and his friend climbed onto the roof of their car. Then the car began to move.

"We jumped off the car into the mud and

were carried along. The mud was like hot bath water. It was like being inside a washing machine full of mud, sticks, and logs."

Suddenly, his friend was sucked under. "Her head was caught between two logs. All I could see was her nose. I grabbed her hair and pulled her up."

Three quarters of a mile downstream, they managed to drag themselves out, injured but safe.

As the mud flowed, it picked up houses and cattle, horses and tractors. People who watched from high ground described the refrigerators, the sofas, the bridges, the roofs that raced by them in the river of mud. Some people watched their houses and cars float away. Others watched as the mud crawled up the walls of their homes and entered through the windows. More than 300 houses were damaged.

The sheriffs' departments and the National Guard evacuated more than 3,000 residents. "Evacuate! Evacuate! Muck is coming!" screamed the sheriffs through their bullhorns.

The people who were able, drove out. Others

were rescued by helicopter. Many lost their lives.

More about the mud

- "I knew it was time to leave when a house and several cars floated past my house."

- "We left when the mud began oozing around the building. When we came back, the house looked like a giant had jumped on it."

- One man drove to the place where his house had been and found nothing but mud.

"It's hard to believe," he said. "The only thing I have left is the shirt on my back and the pants that I'm wearing."

- Thousands of people were evacuated from mud-devastated homes. And thousands of others helped take care of the evacuees. Families and grocery stores donated food. Churches and schools donated space. People offered their homes, their beds, their floors. One man described his living room floor as "wall to wall sleeping bags."

• Most of the men who live in the river valleys are loggers. They work at the logging camps that dot the mountain. One evening, as a group of families sat around at one refugee center, a woman voiced what many were thinking. "Thank God it happened on Sunday and the loggers were home."

Moving ash cloud from Mount St. Helens towers several miles into the air.

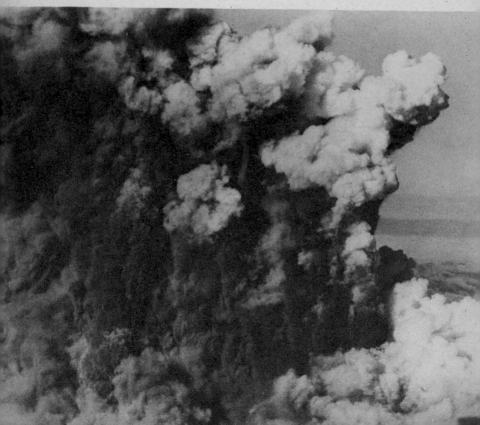

The Ash

When Mount St. Helens blew, 1.3 billion cubic yards of ash shot into the sky — enough to supply every person in the world with more than a ton of ash. If all that ash were packed into one square mile, the pile would be three times as tall as the Empire State building.

Volcanic ash is crushed, pulverized rock. It looks like gray powder. If you blow on it, it puffs into the air like dust. But it is neither powder nor dust. The harmless-looking ash is actually sharp little slivers of glass. Under a microscope you can see that the ash has jagged edges. And if you rub it between your fingers, you can feel that it's hard.

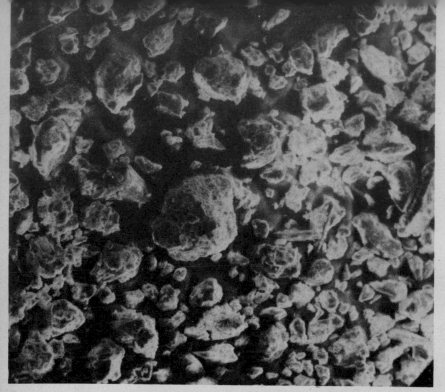

Volcanic dust (ash), magnified 200 times, shows sharp edges of particles that cut up fish gills and irritated eyes and lungs.

When the ash shot up 12 miles into the air, it also billowed out and covered the mountain with a gray-black cloud, a cloud so thick that the sun disappeared.

"It was as dark as the darkest night you've ever seen," said one sheriff.

Many of the people who were on the mountain were suffocated by the ash. Others died from the intense heat and poisonous gases that accompanied the ash.

David Crockett, a TV cameraman, survived. He was at the bottom of the mountain when he heard a roar and saw a wall of mud and a giant cloud coming towards him. Luckily, the mud took a path away from him. But he was enveloped by the cloud of ash. Suddenly, his world turned black.

As Crockett tried to find his way out of the darkness, he spoke into his sound camera.

"I am walking toward the only light I can see. I can hear the mountain rumble. At this very moment I have to say, 'I believe I am dead.' The ash in my eyes burns my eyes, burns my eyes! . . . It's very, very hard to breathe and very dark. If I could only breathe air. Just give me a breath! . . . Ash is coming down on me heavily. It's either dark or I am dead. God, I want to live!" Ten hours later, Crockett was rescued by a helicopter.

On the other side of the mountain, a group of workers were planting trees.

"It was a clear blue day," said one of the crew. "But suddenly it got very dark and the trees and the logs started to shake. The wind was blowing. There were lightning flashes. In less than five seconds the entire mountain was covered with ash. I've never seen anything like it!''

Another member of the crew remembers, "In less than a minute the clouds covered us and the lightning was jumping from cloud to cloud over our heads.''

It wasn't only the people on the mountain that were affected by the ash. As the billowing cloud moved with the wind northeastward across the sky, it "turned day into night" for hundreds of towns in its path.

One man was working in his apple orchard 85 miles east of Mount St. Helens, when the cloud arrived.

"The sky got so dark I thought it was a hailstorm coming. Then I thought it was a locust invasion. Then it got deathly still and all I could see through the dark was an eerie, purplish glow from the sheet lightning. It wasn't until I smelled the sulphur that I knew the mountain had blown."

Another farmer reported that when day became night, the birds went to sleep.

Miles from the mountain, a pilot was dusting crops. Suddenly the dark cloud surrounded his plane and blinded him. He crashed into a pole and was killed.

The black cloud moved along, burying town after town in ash and darkness, and causing automatic street lights to turn themselves on.

The streets of Yakima, Wash., were dark at 1 P.M. on May 18. The few people who ventured out wore masks.

In one town, a baseball team was in the middle of a game when the cloud of ash arrived.

"It was so weird. The sky went all black. First, we were going to finish the game under lights, but pretty soon it was too dark even for that." It was the first ballgame ever to be cancelled because of volcanic ash.

Masked ballplayer. The Yakima Valley College team finally called the game—because of ashfall.

The ash did more than just block out the sun. It fell — like a blizzard of dirty snow.

Drivers were blinded. They couldn't see two feet ahead of their cars. Even their brightest headlights didn't help. Highways were closed and thousands of stranded motorists piled into hotels, motels, churches, schools, and even strangers' houses.

The blizzard of ash drifts like snow but stings much worse than snowflakes.

When the blizzard ended, the cars were still in trouble. There was ash dust everywhere, flurrying around like dust on a dry dirt road. It penetrated air filters and stalled the engines. Some government vehicles tried special filters that were made for use during sandstorms in the Arabian desert. The ash, finer than sand, got through.

Masked and scarved patient and nurse near ash-heaped car outside a hospital.

One of the few tricks that worked was pantyhose tied around the filter. When word got out that pantyhose was a solution to the filter problem, stores sold out immediately.

The most logical solution to the car problem was to stay home, but state patrol cars didn't have that option. They were out under the worst conditions. When the cars returned to the shop, they were a mess.

"We brought in one car that had more than 450 pounds of dust on and in it . . . and I mean in it," said one official. "Behind the glass on dashboard instrument gauges, through brake seals and cylinders and in the brake fluid . . . everywhere. Once you've run a car in those conditions for any amount of time, it's shot."

Cars weren't the only machines that had trouble. Planes couldn't fly; trucks couldn't drive their routes; buses couldn't run. Air-conditioners, washing machines, vacuum cleaners, lawn mowers — all machines with intricate parts — were disabled.

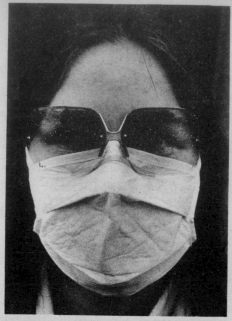
Hospital masks were a fast-selling item.

And the people didn't fare much better. They were advised to stay home. If they had to go out, they wore masks — hospital masks, handkerchief masks, masks made from coffee filters and rubber bands. During the ashiest days, dust masks were being shipped into Washington at the rate of 150,000 a day.

It was hard to get away from the ash. It got into people's eyes and ears. One woman caught in an ash blizzard said:

"I felt like somebody popped my eyeballs

out and rolled them around in a sandbox."

The ash felt gritty in people's mouths, grimy in their hair.

The ash was impossible to clean up. Sweeping didn't help at all. It just sent the ash flying

Even the shrubbery had to be swept clean of the sharp particles of ash.

again. And it was impossible to squirt away the ash with a hose. When it was wet, the ash just bunched up and sat there, like wet cement.

The only solution was to wet it down, shovel it into piles, and cart away the piles. If the piles were left to dry, the ash would scatter again.

For years after the ashfall, the hardest-hit towns would still be cleaning up.

Shoveling the driveway is a dusty job.

(*Above*) Ash had to be shoveled and swept off roofs. (*Below*) Streetcleaners wore masks and caps.

A wedding goes off on schedule in Yakima, Wash.—but the bride and groom wear masks.

A surplus army mask becomes fashionable attire in Portland, Oregon.

More about the ash

• One of the banks in Yakima, Washington, was worried about masked robbers hiding out among the masked people. It put up a sign: For security purposes, please remove your mask before entering.

• A few days after the ash-fall, many hardware stores were sold out of brooms, shovels, hoses, and sprinklers.

• A college student in need of a job went into business cleaning out ash-clogged rain gutters. He charged as much as $25 per job and earned about $125 a day.

• Police in some towns, unable to use their cars, rode around on bicycles.

• In one town in Washington, three feet of ash accumulated in 90 minutes.

• Some small towns in Washington had to borrow street cleaning equipment from Portland and Seattle.

• A passenger jet was forced to land when the fine particles of ash clogged its engine. It had flown for only four minutes through the ash cloud.

• Trucks using CB radios led caravans of cars down ash-filled highways. The trucks traveled two or three across and at five miles an hour. Some caravans were more than a mile long.

• When Mount St. Helens exploded, the ash-cloud showed up on the National Weather Service radar. A piece of the radar screen blazed white "like a piece of pie."

• The biggest particles of ash fell immediately to the ground. The medium-sized particles fell during the following two weeks. The tiniest particles stayed in the stratosphere at an altitude of more than 55,000 feet. Scientists predicted that the tiny particles would filter the sun's rays and cause beautiful sunsets for more than two years.

A terrifying ash cloud descends on Richland, Wash., 130 miles east of Mount St. Helens. May 18 was black Sunday for many Washington towns.

The Animals

There were very few people who lived on Mount St. Helens. And most of those who did were evacuated when the volcano began sputtering. But there was no way to evacuate the millions of animals, no way to pack them up and move them out of the danger zone. When Mount St. Helens blew, the loss of animal life was enormous.

Animals in the line of the blast were wiped out. One biologist talked about some mountain goats that the Forest Service had put on the mountain several years earlier.

"They lived in the blast zone," he said. "I'm sure they were vaporized."

And so were thousands of insects, rodents, rabbits, snakes, and other small animals.

Fish were wiped out by the thousands. Some were seen leaping out of the boiling waters. Others were trapped when the mud filled their streams and rivers.

Even the fish that survived were endangered. A Forest Service biologist, examining the gills of an apparently healthy fish, pointed out to a newspaper reporter:

"See those nicks and jagged edges and the pale color? The ash is cutting up their gills. . . . They'll never make it."

A fish hatchery near the town of Toutle was flooded with mud and ash. More than 10 million baby salmon were destroyed.

Birds were especially hard hit. Many were killed in the blast. Others, in the ash.

When the eruption was over, the barren slopes of Mount St. Helens were gray and lifeless. But several months later, a scientist reported that he had seen some tiny green shoots popping through the ash. Perhaps they were

Much of the desolation in the beautiful wildlife areas around Mount St. Helens was caused by mile-wide mudflows.

a sign that someday the mountain would once again be a forest, teeming with life.

Washington State's Department of Game, Approximate Wildlife Losses

5,250 Roosevelt elk
6,000 blacktailed deer
  200 black bear
  100 mountain goats
   15 mountain lions
44,177 salmon and steelhead trout
One and a half million birds and small animals

More about the animals

- As the mud raced down the mountain, it splattered all around. Birds fell from the air when the mud splashed onto their wings.

- Ash and mud clogged the gills of many fish and caused them to suffocate.

- A rescue party searching for survivors heard some strange squeaking noises. They followed the noises and discovered a dog with three newborn puppies — all in good condition.

• The job of searching for bodies that were buried in ash on the mountain was nearly impossible. The most successful searcher turned out to be Hauser, a two-and-one-half-year-old

German shepherd is patient if not very happy when his master fits a respirator over his muzzle.

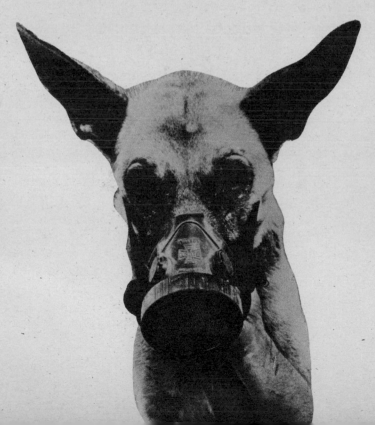

German shepherd. The dog sniffed as his handler walked alongside of him. Many bodies that would never have been found were discovered by Hauser.

• Two men tried to rescue their horses from three-foot-deep mud. They managed to get one horse out, but the horse became frightened and ran back to join the others, just as a log-jam broke. The three horses were swept away in the current.

• One man, about to be rescued by helicopter, shouted, "Wait a minute," and ran back to his house. He came out with his pet boa constrictor.

Studying a Volcano

When Mount St. Helens woke up, geologists were very excited. Finally they would have a chance to study a live volcano on home ground. They rushed to the state of Washington from all over the country. Their job: to figure out what the volcano was doing and to try to predict what it was going to do next.

First, the geologists warned people of the dangers of a big volcanic eruption. It was hard to imagine that the beautiful, snow-covered mountain was going to explode, but with the volcano hissing and spitting and coughing up, the people and the government listened:

1. The mountain was evacuated.
2. The Red Zone was set up.
3. The waters of a reservoir were lowered so that a mudflow would not make it overflow.

On April 3, geologists from the U.S. Geological Survey office issued a warning bulletin that was introduced by a statement intended to discourage panic:

This bulletin is from the U.S. Geological Survey and is for planning purposes. It is not intended to mean that a major volcanic eruption is imminent.

What the bulletin stated is on the following pages.

What To Do When a Volcano Erupts

Most Important — Don't panic, keep calm.

If volcanic ash begins to fall heavily:

Stay indoors

If you are outside, seek shelter, such as a car or building

If you cannot find shelter, breathe through a cloth, such as a handkerchief, preferably a damp cloth to filter out the ash

When air is full of ash, keep your eyes closed as much as possible

Heavy falls of ash seldom last more than a few hours; only rarely do they last a day or more.

A heavy fall of ash may cause darkness during daylight hours, and may temporarily interfere with telephone, radio, and television communication.

Do not try to drive a car during a heavy fall of ash. The chance of an accident will be increased by poor visibility.

A thick accumulation of ash could increase the load on roofs, and saturation of ash by rain could be an additional load. Ash should be removed from flat or low-pitched roofs to prevent a thick accumulation.

Valleys that head at a volcano may be the routes of mudflows, which carry boulders and resemble wet, flowing concrete.

Mudflows can move faster than you can walk or run, but you can drive a car down a valley faster than a mudflow will travel.

When driving along a valley that heads on a volcano, watch up the river channel and parts of the valley floor for the occurrence of mudflows.

Before crossing a highway bridge, look upstream. Do not cross a bridge while a mudflow is moving beneath it.

The danger from a mudflow increases as you approach a river channel, and decreases as you move to higher ground.

Risk from mudflows also decreases with increasing distance from a volcano.

If you become isolated, do not stay near the river channel — move upslope.

Hazards are greatest at the volcano itself, and diminish with increasing distance: *During an eruption, move away from a volcano, not toward it.*

A grim reminder of a volcano's destructive power: Sheriff and military personnel carry out one of the bodies found along a campsite that was in line with the blast.

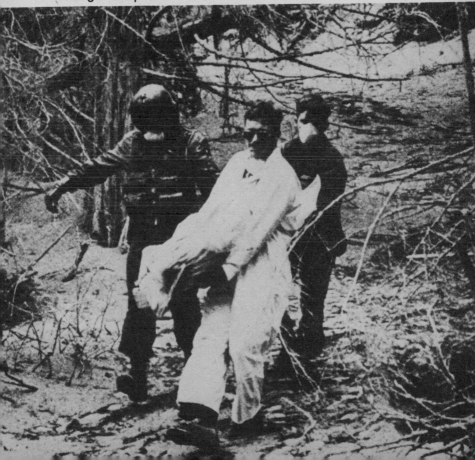

Once the geologists had warned the people of the dangers, they tried to figure out what was happening inside the mountain and what was going to happen.

The scientists used machines to help them collect facts. *Seismographs* measured earthquakes. Seismographs also recorded harmonic tremors, the long rumbles from inside the mountain that mean the magma is moving up the throat of the volcano.

David Johnston, one of those missing after the blast, uses a cospec to measure sulfur dioxide gas emissions from Mount St. Helens.

Tiltmeters told the scientists that the mountain was tilting as the magma moved.

Special *infrared film* told of temperature changes on the surface of the mountain.

Other equipment helped the scientists to analyze the gases that the volcano was expelling.

Geologists hoped that when the volcano was ready to blow, the machines would record a warning: perhaps the earthquakes would get bigger, the harmonic tremors longer, the gases more varied. Perhaps the temperature of the mountain would heat up.

They hoped the mountain would send out some signal that would be a clue. But all they could do was hope.

In the end, the volcano didn't cooperate. There were no warnings, or at least none that the scientists detected. On the morning that Mount St. Helens blew, no one knew until it was too late.

The biggest surprise of all was the sideways explosion — the big blast. Volcanoes usually explode into the sky. They rarely explode sideways. If geologists had even suspected that the volcano might shoot sideways from the big bulge, geologist David Johnston would never have been camped where he was.

It is strange that the volcano gave no warning. Some scientists have suggested that the earthquakes that sent the north slope crashing down the mountain, forced the volcano to blow before it was ready. Perhaps, if the earthquakes hadn't occurred, the volcano would have taken its time and given some signals when "the big one" was ready.

People will be studying Mount St. Helens for years and years, not only the May 18 eruption, but also the eruptions that happened later. For Mount St. Helens did not go back to sleep after May 18, 1980. It erupted many more times.

Science will learn many things from the study of Mount St. Helens. But perhaps the scariest lesson of all is that volcanoes don't follow the rules.

Mount St. Helens in July, 1980. Its beautiful, snowy cone is completely blasted away, leaving an enormous, steaming crater. By the end of October a lava dome, 155 feet high and 900 feet across, had formed in the center of the crater.

Photo sequence taken by amateur photographer Vern Hodgson on Sunday, May 18, 1980, from 15 miles away. Sequence was over a 4-minute period, beginning at 8:30

1

3

A.M. Third photo taken as the bulge began to slide.
Fourth shows cloud filled with ash, hot rocks, and steam.
It is 20 miles across and moving fast.

2

4

Other U.S. Volcanoes

"Whoever thought about something like a volcano, for heaven's sake?" said a resident of Portland, Oregon, several weeks after the May 18th blast. "I mean, this is the United States. Everyone knows that volcanoes are exotic things that are supposed to happen to other parts of the world. . . ."

For most people, the Mount St. Helens eruption was a big surprise. Until Mount St. Helens blew its top, the only active volcanoes in the United States were in Hawaii and Alaska. The last volcano to erupt in the connected United States had been Lassen Peak in Northern California. And that happened in 1915.

Lassen Cinder Cone seen across painted dunes, Lassen Volcanic National Park, Calif. Lassen Peak last erupted in 1915.

But volcanoes are hardly new to the 48 states. Long before there were people, billions of years ago, there were volcanoes — spitting, exploding, and spilling lava and ash all over the country. Volcanic activity created our most beautiful mountains and valleys, lakes and islands, and rocky cliffs. The ash from these ancient volcanoes provided the mineral-rich soil for the forests and farms of today.

Hot rock, like that which once flowed from those ancient volcanoes, still lies under the continent. Where that molten rock heats the water in the earth, there are "hot spots" or steam vents. The most famous of these hot spots is in Yellowstone National Park. There, a hot-water fountain, or geyser, named Old Faithful, shoots up into the sky at regular intervals. The hot springs and bubbling mud ponds in Yellowstone, and in many other places in the United States, are evidence that once there were violently erupting volcanoes charring and changing the landscape.

Minerva Terrace, Mammoth Hot Springs, Yellowstone, showing steam and travertine deposits.

Old Faithful, the famous steam geyser in Yellowstone National Park, erupts at regular intervals.

Closeup of pumice rocks (porous lava) hurled into the Toutle riverbed from Mount St. Helens on May 18.

Volcanic rocks have been found in nearly every one of the United States, but in recent geologic time (the past few million years), the western part of the country has been the most active, volcanically — especially the Cascade Mountains in Washington, Oregon, and Northern California.

Most of the Cascade Mountains were once active volcanoes. Mount St. Helens is part of the Cascade range. Since Mount St. Helens erupted, scientists have been studying the other mountains in the Cascades.

(Above) Mount Rainier, highest point in Washington, is 14,410 feet high. (Below) Beautiful Mount Shasta in California is 14,162 feet high.

Within the last 70 years, Mount Lassen and Mount St. Helens have erupted. Mount Baker and Mount Rainer in Washington, and Mount Shasta in California, have spurted steam and perhaps even ash. And shortly after the Mount St. Helens eruption, there was a flurry of earthquakes at Mount Hood in Oregon.

The activity in these mountains is probably not an indication that the volcanoes are waking up. But geologists are watching.

It will be years before geologists understand exactly why Mount St. Helens blew so unexpectedly on May 18, 1980. But they learned from that eruption. They were able to "read" the earthquakes, the harmonic tremors, and the other signs of imminent eruption, and to predict some of the other Mount St. Helens eruptions later in the year.

Mount St. Helens has erupted a number of times in the past one thousand years. Those eruptions damaged forests and wildlife just as the one in 1980 did. But in earlier times, there weren't large, populated areas nearby that could be affected. Now, geologists must reckon on the important *people* factor. Hopefully, some very important and life-saving lessons have been learned from the experiences of Mount St. Helens' 1980 blast.

Sunset Crater, Arizona. This cinder cone in the desert is another reminder that there have been volcanoes in other parts of continental United States besides the Cascades.

Two of about 36 active volcanoes in Alaska: *(above)* Katmai steams from its snow-capped crater. *(Below)* Aniakchak Crater in Aniakchak National Monument Park. The area was devastated by the erupting volcano in 1931.

Facts about Mount St. Helens

Name: Indians called it "Smoking Mountain." Renamed for Baron St. Helens; in 1790, he averted war between England and Spain over water rights at Vancouver Island.

Location: Southwestern Washington, about 45 miles northeast of Portland, Oregon.

Historic activity: Ancient volcanic center may be 36,000 years old. Spasmodic eruptions at intervals over past 4,500 years. Considered potentially dangerous long before the 1980 blast.

Statistics on 1980 eruption:

Height of mountain at top:
  before March 27: 9,677 feet.
  after May 18: 8,260 feet.

Height of north slope:
  before May 18: 9,200 feet
  after May 18: 6,100 feet

Height of May 18 eruption: 65,000 feet, or about 12 miles into the sky.

Amount of ash spewed: 1.3 billion cubic yards (about the same as famous Vesuvius eruption that buried Pompeii in 79 A.D.).

Cloud size (4 minutes after eruption began): over 20 miles wide.

Duration of eruption: 9 hours.

Composition of exploding material: steam, poisonous gases, rock, pumice (frothy lava), ice blocks, pyroclastic (glasslike) ash.

Energy output: between 10 and 50 megatons of TNT (about the same force as that released by largest nuclear bomb test, conducted by USSR in 1961).

Photo credits (number indicates page)

Burlington Lines: 73.
NASA: 36.
National Park Service: 72
Northern Pacific Railway: 4.
Spence Air Photos: 75, 77.
UPI: 9, 25, (below) 28, 48, 49, 57, 63, 74, 79.
U.S. Dept. of the Interior: 71, (above) 78.
U.S. Geological Survey: 6, 12, 19, 21, 22, 34, 64.
Visions: Bockwinkel/Visions: 42. Smith/Visions: 38, 40, 41, 45, 46, 47.
Wide World: 11, 24, (above) 28, 52, 67, (with Hodgson/Everett Wash. Herald) 68-9, (below) 78.
Woodfin Camp: Werth/Woodfin Camp: 17, 30, 44, 55.